BRAINPOWER

*Discover How to Sharpen
Your Mind, Improve
Working Memory,
and Use More of Your
Brain Capacity*

by Chadwick Brevard

Table of Contents

Introduction

Let me start with a simple statement: The myth that humans only use 10% of their brains is utterly absurd. In fact, through the course of a normal day, most people use almost every portion of their brain. Therefore, this book doesn't intend to somehow activate a magical "other" 90% which would turn you into a genius savant overnight. That's because, like every other portion of the body, the brain is a massive, living organ. The neurons in your brain are constantly drawing nutrients and thriving. Therefore, there *is no* 90% left over to activate, that will all of a sudden transform you into a grand intellectual at the drop of a hat.

However, here's the catch: While you use 100% of your brain over the course of a day, there are periods of time when the brain activity of different portions may be significantly lower that it could or should be, on an individual moment-by-moment basis. Therefore, even when you *do* use the entirety of your brain throughout the day, that still doesn't mean that you access the *correct* parts of your brain for the activity at hand. Moreover, nor does it mean that the density of the neural pathways between different portions is high enough to allow you to capitalize on the full potential of the most energy-consuming human organ — the brain, taking up roughly 20% of the human body's energy.

However, fret not, my eager disciple. Whether young or old, the neural pathways in the brain never stop developing, and this propagation of neurons within different sectors of your brain can be intensified at any age — with the right approach and exercises. And that's the *raison d'être* of this book. From here on, I will guide you through a rigorous set of activities that will start boosting your Brainpower and working memory within the first week of training. Furthermore, not only will this book help you improve your short and long-term memory, the exercises will also help you improve your aptitude in association-making, which will significantly further the amount of brain capacity that you are able to access at any given moment.

Can you imagine how much better your life will be if you were to tone up your brain into the leanest, meanest, thought-producing machine it could possibly become? Are you ready to leave behind days of absent-mindedness, and never again experience a thought on the tip of your tongue frustratingly fluttering away just as you're about to utter it? Are you ready to experience the immense potential hiding within the brain of every human being? Then let's get started!

Chapter 1: Understanding Your Enemy

Now, if reading this chapter's title has you confused, let me say it outright—your biggest enemy in this battle is your own brain. After all, the brain is an organ which simply houses our consciousness through a series of chemical reactions and electrical impulses. While the very existence of our consciousness may require that the brain stay operational throughout our lives, it would still prefer to revert to its default state of staying just barely as active as necessary in order to keep the rest of the body up and running.

To use an analogy, the brain is like that guitar you insisted upon as a birthday gift when you were young. If you were among the people who asked and asked for one and then left it rotting on a stand for a decade in your bedroom, it would obviously be horribly out-of-tune, with rusted strings on the verge of snapping, and you would very likely not know how to play it even if you *did* pick it up after all this time. Oh, it would definitely throw out shrieking plucks and groans if played in this state, but you would hardly call that racket "music", would you? Similarly, mastery over your own brain requires active thought and effort.

If you think that the brain's power and functions are limited to analysis, cognition, and memory, let me point out that this is an overly simplistic view of the varied activities taking place in your head at any point of any given day. The list of brain functions concerning thought processes *alone*—excluding any activities concerning bodily functions—count visual working memory, spatial memory, sustained attention, cognition, working memory, verbal memory, serial learning, short-term, long-term, and episodic memory, along with executive function, among many, *many* others.

However, while these functions are diverse and dizzyingly varied, brain exercises often serve to improve several of those at a time. Thus, even if there are roughly twenty or more identifiable metrics to improve in order to boost your Brainpower, they can all be served by incorporating seven or eight different kinds of exercises in your daily and weekly schedules. To give you a sense of the grand scope of the magnificent work performed by the brain through our daily lives, the functions I listed above did not even account for associations within the different portions, the degree of success for which is determined by the density of neural pathways between the portions responsible for each activity. This factor doesn't just arithmetically increase the power of the brain, but rather exponentially blows it up.

To clarify this further, let's tackle the example of problem-solving. From the *simplified* list of functions you need to call upon to find the best way through the situation, you need to exercise your (1) short-term memory to keep every aspect and detail of the situation in mind, (2) sustained attention to focus your mental energies on resolving this issue, (3) long-term memory along with (4) associative functions to compare this problem with a similar situation in the past, (5) episodic memory to recall the circumstances and steps which you took then to resolve the issue, (6) cognition to understand the take-away lesson from both problems as well as to adapt the solution from the past to solve the present problem, and (7) executive function to chalk up a plan of action and carry it through. And this is the *simple* answer for how it all works together.

Now if we add the power of association in the mix, if your neural density is low between your long term and episodic functions, you may recall the occurrence of a previous problem and solution, yet have trouble remembering the specifics. If your associative capabilities between short-term memory and cognition are weak, you may fail to remember all the relevant details pertinent to the problem at hand— which means that you either won't be able to think of all possible options you have to resolve the problem, or won't be able to successfully adapt previous solutions to this occurrence. Now, think of the possibility of the associative powers between most portions in your brain being average or weaker than they should be. The compounding of each negative effect is what will set others with greater Brainpower apart from your eventual conclusion and resolution.

And *that* is the scary—*and redeeming*—nature of the brain. While weaker neural density along associative pathways compound to make small problems significantly larger, working a little bit on improving those associations shows compounded benefits right away as well. Thus, apart from other exercises, you'll devote significant periods of time to improving your associative neural pathways as well.

Chapter 2: How to Improve Brainpower through Reading

As your first exercise, take on as much reading as your schedule would allow. Not only does this give you a chance to either update yourself on the workings of the world, or stretch your imagination as you get lost in some choice fiction, it also improves your short-term memory and sense of cognition, among many others.

The last sentence must have revealed the fact that I don't necessarily need you to stick to non-fiction literary works, if the other choices are more to your liking. However, choosing any literature which either deals with issues comprehensively or that has layered interpretations within its folds would do you more good than reading something straightforward. Within this activity as well, if you choose to read longer works rather than shorter articles, etc., your improvement would be significantly better.

Once you've finished reading, your second exercise right after is to construct unending "thought chains". Although normal chains of thought have a definite start and end, and usually deal with one or comparatively less topics, a thought chain should be different in that you're using it to link several subjects together. The nature or result of the chains doesn't even need to be perspective or serious, as long as you can continue it across various subjects before coming to a close.

As an example, if you've just finished reading "Harry Potter", you could prompt yourself to wonder about the nature of wands, and why specific types of wood allow for greater synchronization with the powers of a wizard or witch. That thought could lead to the possibility of whether any of the specified types of wood were ever considered sacred or powerful by pagan and other religions through the ages, and if that was the source of inspiration for the choices by the author. From that point, you could wonder if those trees are therefore protected under any sort of legal act by the world of wizardry, and if there are any sacred groves which would deliver wands of greater magic than usual. This could turn you down the path of the preservation of forestry, and whether wizard law allows cutting down nature for the purposes of residential encroachment, or to be used as industrial or commercial fuel—which could then lead to the current state of petroleum in the world and if there are any magical methods in the Harry Potter world of replicating or generating petroleum by using wood as the starting product for the spell. This thought chain could then either head towards the necessities of oil in today's age, the kind of magic car you would have liked to drive and why, or even possible legal precedents for illegal deforestation in front of wizarding courts, and many others.

Although this may seem like an absurd example, *that* is precisely the point. You're basically warming up your neural pathways to lead yourself through various diverse topics coming under the umbrella of a single subject of discussion, in preparation for times when you'll seriously need it.

Not only will this exercise improve your brain performance, it would also train you to question and explore every alternative path available to you in any given situation. Moreover, this would also give rise to tangential associative abilities, where you can "think out of the box". In this manner, you get to have fun exploring unanswered questions on hypothetical situations based on your knowledge from real life and also work on the neural density between various portions of your brain in order to improve overall Brainpower.

Chapter 3:   The Value and Practice of Meditation and Mindfulness

Meditative exercises have long since been held in great esteem as a powerful way of conquering and controlling one's own brain. That's primarily because nowhere else is the understanding of your brain being your own biggest enemy more clearly visible than during the onslaught of errant thoughts assaulting you in the very moments when you're trying to focus and quiet all sources of distraction in your head.

Since there are many different forms of meditation, for our purposes, they're simply a means to an end. Therefore, I'm going to limit our discussion to what you need to practice intently to improve Brainpower, which is **"mindfulness"** meditation. Use the power of this exercise to block all thoughts which you didn't initiate yourself, in exchange for the calm feeling of belonging in the moment while you quietly experience the *feel* of your own body.

To start mindfulness meditation, find a quiet spot at home for fifteen minutes of your day, and sit in a comfortable position. While traditional meditative poses often include a cross-legged seated position, you're free to choose any spot or position where you're comfortable and won't fall asleep. However, no matter how you sit, touch your index fingers to your thumbs while keeping the rest of the hand loosely open, and place it palms-upward on your knees.

While you may play some soothing music in the background if you are in a noisy environment, the ideal way to perform this would still be in complete silence. Close your eyes and start inhaling and exhaling deeply. If you're a neophyte in meditative practices, start by counting each inhalation to the tune of one to five Mississippi's. Hold your breath to the count of three, and then exhale again for five counts. Keep a steady rhythm without break, and simply concentrate on your breath and the count. Once an unbroken rhythm is achieved, pay attention to the way your body feels with every cycle of breathing. Concentrate on the feeling of your lungs, the sounds of air rushing in and out, the muscles of your body through each cycle, etc. Push away any unnecessary thoughts which aren't related to the exercise at hand. Continue this for at least fifteen to twenty minutes once a day.

When you have practiced and achieved sufficient meditative prowess to exert some measure of control over your thoughts, and have understood the techniques of brushing away anything from your head which you didn't actively call upon yourself, you are ready to start on the second phase of this exercise.

Once you believe you have achieved some sort of intermediate control over your thoughts, you're going to engage in visualization exercises. For this, schedule at least half an hour at the end of your day, and create an atmosphere similar to the mindfulness meditation. After you're seated comfortably, relax and think back on your entire day. And I do mean, the *whole* day. This is going to be an extremely challenging endeavor, but will immeasurably boost your Brainpower once you're able to even *somewhat* accomplish this objective.

Right off the bat, think about the time when you woke up and started your day. Try and recreate the exact scenario in your mind, and walk through your morning as you got ready for work, studies, daily chores, etc. Use your mind to visualize the scenes as if they are videos playing on the insides of your eyelids. Try and recall the different colors, shapes, and smells, the exact sequence of events from you getting up to you getting ready for the next phase of your day, the feel and taste of the toothpaste in your mouth, the conversations you had in the meanwhile, etc. From there on, move to the second part of your day and so on until you can recreate your daily experiences up to the point where you are starting this meditative exercise.

Now, I'm going to be completely honest with you—for most, this exercise will be impossible to complete in the first few months at the very least, even with rigorous practice. While you'll recall significant moments from your day, and even the list of foods which you consumed, trying to recreate exact chains of events—complete with sensory data—is a feat which will take *rigorous* dedication to achieve. But, that's the general idea, and the requirement level for what you wish to achieve.

In exchange, once you're able to accomplish this feat, what you'll receive is an *insane* boost in your short- and long-term memory, as well as a finely honed ability to focus on any detail from your past. You'll also find that your memory of events and situations dictating your life from the point you start this exercise will *significantly* improve, and that you'll gain the ability to even recall smaller and seemingly insignificant details as time passes. For 45 minutes a day, this achievement is nothing less than a veritable cheat-code to handling the ups and downs of life.

Chapter 4: Turning Distractions into an Advantage

Now, while we constantly aim at removing distractions from our surroundings, their ever-present existence is unavoidable in 21st century life. What with smaller houses and busier metropolitan cities, distractions are part and parcel of modern living. And the bigger point to make is—the brain conclusively does *not* work better in the absence of any distractions.

Extensive research has already proven that cognition does not thrive in the utter absence of any distraction whatsoever, but rather peaks with a sweet-spot of distracting sounds and occurrences from one's background. The same studies concluded that to achieve peak creativity and out-of-the-box thinking, which is basically a jumble of associative and cognitive functions that either adapt pre-existing knowledge from other fields of application to the present one, *some* levels of distraction present surmountable obstacles that force the brain to connect dots so it works *around* the problem at hand rather than try to unsuccessfully force its way *through* it.

Another confirmed finding is that distractions provide a way for the brain to buckle down and hone its focus on a singular problem of your choosing, rather than being distracted through the plethora of errant thoughts which burst through when working against a backdrop of complete silence. Thus, this becomes a handy cheat for you to employ when you're tackling problems where you can't find a satisfactory way through. Instead of trying to bolt yourself in a cone of silence to come up with answers to the predicament at hand, play some music from genres that you would never listen to in a million years—albeit at a volume no higher than 75 decibels or so. While doing so in a time of crisis will force your brain to come up with creative solutions, practicing such methods regularly will further help you sharpen your mental discipline, so that you can exert your complete attention on any matter at hand when required—instead of being distracted as easily as a stoner sniffing out the smell of freshly-baked cookies in the air.

In such a manner, while this method will largely serve as a way of boosting your Brainpower when needed in the short term without any significant improvement to your neural pathways, it will nonetheless help you wield your existing significant mental capabilities *exactly* as you order them. After all, the fine point of a scalpel is more useful as a cutting tool than a blunt hammer.

Chapter 5: Adopting the Principles of Lifelong Learning and Continuous Improvement

Whether fortunately or otherwise, the brain often functions like other muscles in our body—if we fail to exercise any portion for any significant periods of time, it will atrophy. In this case, that means you lose neural density in the unused parts of the brain.

This is an important point to remember, because it points to the fact that giving in to mental and intellectual stagnation means dulling the corresponding areas of your brain. Therefore, in order to counter that, you need to constantly keep adding new skill sets—and not just general knowledge—to your list of .competencies.

However, out of all the possibilities which may help you boost your Brainpower, the most significantly helpful one is to learn a new language. This particular exercise may seem strange to those who have never attempted to learn languages which don't immediately surround them, but the development of this skill requires the involvement of most of your cognitive functions. Think about it for a moment, in order to learn a new language—you need to learn the sounds of the words, their meanings, then compare them to meanings of parallel words in your language in order to remember them, exert structure upon them in the form of grammar, use episodic experiences from your period of learning to remember relevant or appropriate responses in different situations, use cognition to formulate new sentences of your own which is a feat that requires associative recall from all of the other sections on which you've been working, and so on and so forth.

In choosing a new language to learn, pick languages that have the least in common with the one which you speak. Therefore, instead of picking French to supplement your native English, choose Russian or one of the other Slavic tongues. Alternatively, you can also go for Japanese or Chinese as a viable option. This immensity of difference in languages is vital because it increases the factor of difficulty involved in learning it. And the more difficult the task, the greater the improvement upon the capabilities of your brain. This task is also made ridiculously convenient through easily available free apps such as DuoLingo.

Furthermore, another language which you should compulsorily pick up if you're truly intent on improving your intellectual capacity is the language of music. And yes, it's a language of its own, complete with written and spoken components, its own sense of grammatical structure, etc. Basically, learn a musical instrument. If you've already learnt one, then follow the same principle as above—choose a secondary instrument which is as different from your original choice as possible.

Involving yourself in the creation of music has twice the benefits. Not only are you involving every auditory, muscular, and cognitive function which would have been involved in the language exercise, but you're developing additional auditory and cognitive senses for the interpretation of music as per that instrument. Also, depending on the choice of instrument, you work on additional portions of your brain as well—either those involved with dexterity, speed of reflexes to keep up with tempo, or improved control over your muscles for efficient breath exertion, etc.

Significant studies have researched the effects of music on the brain. Their findings have been quite illuminating in that—unlike developed languages—music seems to have a direct effect on the emotional systems of the brain. Therefore, when you're creating your own music rhythms, you're not only exercising the intellectual parts of your brain which would allow you to play with the language of music, but you're also strengthening associative cognition between the logic and emotional sectors of your brain.

Chapter 6: Everyday Games for Boosting Brainpower

Aside from the exercises and objectives in the previous chapters, there's another fun way for you to enhance your Brainpower—and that is by playing games. Regardless of your age, depending on the choice of game, you work on several prime functions of your brain—such as executive decision-making, reflexes, rapid associations, strategic planning, etc, not to mention several others, useful in everyday life, such as hand-eye coordination and so on.

Therefore, whether you're 15 or 55, you need to set some time aside—even only an hour or two every week—to engage in some gaming of your own. Now, by gaming, I don't mean you need to log in to Battlefield 4 or World of Warcraft—though they have their own merits as well. Instead, what I mean are some good old-fashioned rounds of chess, jigsaw puzzles, etc.

From the two mentioned above, speed chess is great for developing strategic association and cognitive planning, and calls upon diverse functions to beat an opponent. On the other hand, jigsaw puzzles develop spatial memory and cognitive functions, among many others. Since each of them can be played alone (with chess against a computer), these are great ways of taking some time off on different days of the week, while still productively exercising your brain for the purposes of overall improvement.

If you're not the biggest fan of either of those options, you can also indulge in a game of Sudoku or Crosswords every day, or even some Scrabble. Each of these games, while simple in themselves, train diverse areas of your brain *very* effectively—and essentially allow you to pull the stops and visualize several possibilities simultaneously when under pressure. Not only do they improve your sense of recall, as well as pattern recognition and numerical or linguistic cognition, but they hone your ability to identify the various options available to you in a situation at any given point of time. After all, you can only reason out the solution to any problem in your day when you have the capacity to see all the options available for you.

Of course, the definition of "game" varies from person to person, and some may wish to take up IQ tests as a form of gaming as well. Although there are myriads of such tests available online, IQ tests by themselves are never accurate methods of determining the Intelligence Quotient of a person. The function which they *do* serve well is that of testing cognition and recall under duress. Furthermore, if you attempt to retake tests, not only will you improve upon your short-term memory in a bid to answer previously incorrect questions more accurately, but will also expand your cognitive understanding of the subject matter at hand. Besides, plenty of neurological experts swear by solving some math problems every day to keep your brain well-honed, so this perfectly fits the bill.

Finally, the miracle of technology has granted us the ability to carry around several truck-loads worth of reading materials and brain development resources in one small cell-phone. And so we finally touch upon the wondrous and convenient world of brain-training apps. Through easy-to-use and freely available apps such as Fit Brains Trainer, Brain Trainer Special, Lumosity, etc., you can now get your daily dose of mental improvement requirements by engaging in exercises which work on memory, attention span, cognitive capabilities under pressure, thought flexibility, etc. Many among such games even provide additional impetus to work harder by way of live competitions between two players, thus pushing your brain to perform more efficiently than it would have under relaxed conditions. The great part about this is that the capacity of a brain doesn't depend on the average performance in relaxed states, but rather on the peak output exerted under minimal to maximum duress. Since most conditions and scenarios which bear serious thought present some stakes worth taking seriously anyway, as the maximum output under pressure rises, so does the overall capability of your brain.

Conclusion

While we've discussed several methods of boosting your Brainpower in this book, by no means are these the only ones out there capable of providing your desired result of greater access to improved mental functions. Among the various options easily available to you for example, the simplest is to take better care of your body.

While I'm not going to ask you to stop drinking sodas or eating junk foods outright, one simple habit that you *can* inculcate is to sleep at least six to eight hours every day. Put simply, lack of sleep puts a severe dent in your short-term recall as well as associative functions. Given that most people decide to stay up and cram on nights before important exams or presentations, this habit is ignored more often than people think—even though everyone already understands its value.

Furthermore, even if you don't wish to drastically alter your eating habits, you should include more fish in your diet. Also, if you cook at home, use olive oil in your cuisine in order to boost your mental functions. Studies have proven that Mediterraneans who regularly include olive oil and seafood in their diet show 36% less neurological deterioration than their global counterparts. Include a small handful of cashew or almonds within your daily food intake as well. Research shows that magnesium directly improves brain function, and the list of high magnesium foods include nuts, fish, bananas, dark chocolate, etc. Lastly, don't exceed more than 3 cups of coffee in a day. While caffeine helps to temporarily boost brain function, excessive consumption will just leave you drained, dehydrated, and unfocused. Any more than that quantity per day is bad for your heart.

Exercise has long been proven as an effective method to boost brain function as well. Not only does toning yourself up into better shape protect your cardiovascular system, and release endorphins which promote a healthier frame of mind, but it also increases blood supply to the brain, and induces production of compounds which reduce the chances of neural degeneration. Lastly, you can also ensure that you get plenty of exposure to sunlight, with UV blockers on, of course. Vitamin D receptors induce neural development in the brain, and so are vital in the healthy formation of areas dealing with memory and cognitive processing.

As you can see, there are innumerable options open if you wish to boost your Brainpower. However, if you diligently apply yourself to every exercise included in here alone, I can guarantee that you will rapidly boost your mental capabilities by leaps and bounds into leagues which you wouldn't have believed possible before. In the end, choose the ones which intrigue you the most, and stick with them before moving on to the other methods listed here. Because, before you feel the thrill of a self-upgraded brain, if you're not having fun while you're at it, it'll soon become a chore. And the essence of a repetitive and mind-numbing chore is the very antithesis of what you're trying to achieve here.

Finally, I'd like to thank you for purchasing this book! If you enjoyed it or found it helpful, I'd greatly appreciate it if you'd take a moment to leave a review on Amazon. Thank you!

20343748R00026

Printed in Great Britain
by Amazon